N O P

Q R S T

U V W

X Y Z

PRINCE

A to Z

Smith Street Books

In the world of pop music, there are few musicians who have stood at the nexus of so many points as Prince: a pioneer of minimalist funk; a seamless blender of jazz, pop and electro; a fluid experimenter with an uncanny understanding of the art of the hit record. Prince existed at that rare intersection of mainstream and experimental – owning the charts, yet remaining relevant, intriguing and important.

His acute ear for melody and pop sensibility combined with a multitude of talents meant that he had broad appeal, way beyond other straight-out funk, jazz or pop acts. He was a multi-instrumentalist with serious guitar skills, nimble piano fingers and was even at home behind a drum kit.

When the world lost Prince in April of 2016, we lost a true one-of-a-kind.

Prince was a purple pop enigma. Is there another major artist so synonymous with a colour? And purple, no less – a colour that is less than popular. Yet Prince somehow made it cool, which was no mean feat. Who else could rock frills, lace, lamé, paisley, polka dots, puffy sleeves, cravats, flared jumpsuits, sequins, studs and a range of eye-searing jewel tones that would make a children's entertainer cringe, and yet he made it look sharp, hip and, most of all, sexy and masculine.

Prince was deeply religious and yet responsible for some of the raunchiest songs to ever grace the pop charts. A vegetarian, gender-fluid fashionista, deeply spiritual believer and sexual adventurer – Prince was a mass of contradictions in life but an incomparable innovator in music. He wasn't afraid to throw the bass out on a funk track – imagine that, funk with no bass! We don't have to because we have 'Kiss' as a testament to how a simple groove can set the charts on fire. The moves! The songs! The suits! A triple-jointed dancer, light on his feet and generous with the hips – Prince could bring any show to life with a twirl, the splits or a gravity-defying toss of the guitar – sometimes all within the same flourish.

Although he was a sexually-charged and extroverted showman on stage, Prince remained elusive and enigmatic in his private life. He was famously shy and reserved in interviews, he had a string of failed relationships and a secret vault holding an almost endless supply of unreleased material. Yet it was this inscrutability that created such a unique space for audiences to feel connection, affinity and impact. Prince addressed his ambiguity in 'Controversy', 'Am I black or white? / Am I straight or gay?' Then in a particularly Prince way, pinpoints his appeal with the most important question: 'Was I what you wanted me to be?' What made Prince controversial then is what defines him today: who he was, what made him different and what makes him unforgettable.

STEVE WIDE

A IS ALSO FOR

Androgyny

Prince rarely spoke about his gender-fluid image, saying he couldn't understand what the fuss was about and that he just liked to dress up. In an interview with Chris Rock he said, 'I think I was just … being who I was. Being the true Gemini that I am.' He said he wore high heels because, 'The girls like them.'

...

Around the World in a Day

The seventh studio album by Prince. Released to a mixed reception, the album eventually became the second *Billboard* number one album for Prince and The Revolution, and spawned two top 10 hits with 'Raspberry Beret' and 'Pop Life'. The psychedelic cover drew comparisons to the Beatles' *Sgt. Pepper's Lonely Hearts Club Band*. Prince denied any influence but stated that he liked the album being called 'psychedelic' because it was the only time in history where songs and colours came together.

...

Apollonia 6

In 1981, Prince formed a three-piece vocal group called Vanity 6, which came to an end after lead singer Vanity (Denise Matthews) left during a legal dispute, also abandoning her role in the movie *Purple Rain*. Patricia Kotero replaced her, and was renamed Apollonia (her middle name) by Prince. The new group, Apollonia 6, had a hit with 'Sex Shooter'.

...

Art Official Age

Prince's 37th studio album, which reached number five on the *Billboard* chart. It was released simultaneously with *Plectrumelectrum* (officially his 36th album), the only LP recorded by Prince with his touring band 3rdeyegirl. *Art Official Age* was released under a renewed deal with Prince's long-time enemy Warner Bros. Records.

'Alphabet St.' has been covered by The Jesus and Mary Chain and Sufjan Stevens.

The video for 'Alphabet St.' features swirling animated letters; those with keen eyes should look out for hidden messages which include various lyrics plus the phrases 'Heaven is so beautiful', 'H is 4 Punks', '4 the Light' and best of all: 'Please don't buy the *Black Album*, I'm sorry'.

Cat Glover became famous after receiving a perfect score on TV talent show *Star Search* with a dance move called The Cat Scat, which she repeated in the video for Prince's 'U Got the Look'.

It has long been rumoured, but never confirmed, that singer Capriccio Caesar is the lovechild of Prince and Cat Glover.

Ween used a sample of the song – Prince screaming 'No!' – at the start of their hit, 'Push th' Little Daisies'.

Arrested Development sampled 'Alphabet St.' on their hit song 'Tennessee'. They were subsequently sued for unauthorised use and had to pay Prince US$100,000.

A
IS FOR
ALPHABET ST

The first single lifted from 1988's *Lovesexy* – and the only track on the album to reach the top 10 (in both the UK and the US) – 'Alphabet St.' holds the distinction of being the first Prince song to be released on compact disc. The sample-heavy track also features rapper, dancer and frequent Prince collaborator Catherine 'Cat' Glover. Put simply, the song is about male-to-female oral sex, but a sly Prince made it obscure enough to get past even the most prurient censors of the day. The B-side of the same name was basically an instrumental, and came with the psychedelic title 'Alphabet St. (This is Not Music, This is a Trip)'.

Following the huge success of the *Purple Rain* soundtrack album, Prince wrote and recorded music for the 1989 film *Batman*, which he released on his 11th studio LP of the same name, along with several songs that never made it to the film (Danny Elfman's score for the film was released separately as *Batman: Original Motion Picture Score*). Prince's second soundtrack album sat at number one on the *Billboard* chart for six weeks straight and featured hit singles 'Batdance', 'Partyman' and 'The Arms of Orion,' featuring Sheena Easton. Director Tim Burton reportedly listened to Prince non-stop during filming, and it's said that Prince's music was a huge influence on Burton's conception of the Joker. The film was a box office hit and Prince was clearly into the project, getting fully into character in his film clip for 'Partyman'. Which character? The iconically purple-clad Joker, of course!

IS FOR

BATMAN

Film producer Mark Canton recalled, 'I brought Prince over to London and you could just tell his kind of genius was in touch with the movie. By the time we had dinner that night, he had three songs in his head. Three weeks later, he had nine songs.'

Prince met Kim Basinger on the set of *Batman*. They reportedly became infatuated with each other and a brief relationship began. Her concerned family turned up to Prince's house one day and whisked her away, but not before they had recorded an (unreleased) album called *Hollywood Affair*, on which she raps 'I'll Be Your Slave,' on a track called 'Color of Sex'.

Despite being a huge Prince fan, director Tim Burton told David Breskin in 1991 that the 'intrusive' soundtrack was the result of an 'unholy alliance' between the director and the studio's marketing plan. Burton said that, '[The music] completely lost me. And it tainted a lot. It tainted something that I don't want to taint, which is how you feel about an artist.'

The first song Prince taught himself to play on the guitar was the 1960s *Batman* TV theme.

The Black Album
Prince's infamous 16th studio album was eventually released in November 1994. Prince's dissatisfaction with Warner Bros. Records' contractual obligations, and with the album itself, led him to stop the original December 1987 release. The promotional copies of the 1987 album featured a black sleeve with only a song listing and catalogue number appearing on the disc itself. When the album was withdrawn, these promos were quickly copied, becoming one of the most sought-after bootlegs in history.

...

Bicycle
A few days before his death, Prince was spotted casually riding his bicycle around his Paisley Park Estate, just hours after he had been released from hospital, reportedly suffering from the flu.

...

The Beautiful Ones
The tentative title of Prince's intended memoir, the story of his life presented in an 'unconventional' and 'poetic' way. It was slated for release by Random House in 2017. At the time of his death only 50 pages had been written.

...

Bootlegs
Prince famously hated bootlegs and bootleggers. A Manhattan record store claimed that he once walked into their store, grabbed all of the Prince bootlegs from the shelf and walked out with them.

...

Backmasking
A sound technique that uses reversed audio, which Prince used in songs 'Dear Nikki' and 'Baby I'm A Star' (in which the backmasking track, played in reverse, reveals the lyrics 'So like, fuck them man! What do they know? / All their taste is in their mouth / Really, what the fuck do they know? / Come on, baby / Let's go crazy!'

C

IS ALSO FOR

'Cream'

Prince's 50th single was lifted from his 13th studio album, *Diamonds and Pearls*. Prince famously said 'Cream' was written while he stood in front of the mirror. His final song to reach number one on the *Billboard* chart, the video was directed by fashion photographer Rebecca Blake, who talked of being amazed at how brilliantly Prince 'moved around in the space she had set' for the clip.

...

Children

Prince had just one son, Ahmir Gregory Nelson, with Mayte Garcia to whom he was married from '96–99. Tragically, Ahmir was born with the rare Pfeiffer Syndrome and died less than a week after his birth. There have been rumours and claims of Prince fathering other children, but nothing has ever been substantiated.

...

Bob Cavallo

Prince's manager, who managed a plethora of acts including Earth, Wind and Fire, Green Day, Weezer, Alanis Morissette and Selena Gomez. Cavallo managed Prince throughout the 80s. Prince wouldn't renew his deal with Cavallo unless he got him a motion picture deal – which led to Cavallo producing *Purple Rain* and *Under the Cherry Moon*.

...

Crystal Ball

The double album *Sign o' the Times*, was originally going to be a triple album called *Crystal Ball*.

...

Camille

Prince sped up vocal tracks on *Sign o' the Times* and attributed them to a female alter ego, who he named Camille. He also wrote the liner notes from the *Lovesexy* tour as a piece of prose with Camille as the main character, and he recorded a whole album, which was never released, as Camille.

The cover of *Controversy* is just a hint at what would be Prince's lifetime link with the colour purple, with his dusty-purple jacket (complete with 'Rude Boy' pin) and the purple type. The pin and the colour of the jacket are echoed in the illustrated writing on the (very purple) cover of *1999*. The iconic *Purple Rain* came shortly after, forever making Prince 'The Purple One'.

In 1981, the *Village Voice* voted *Controversy* eighth-best album of the year.

LCD Sound System covered 'Controversy' at Coachella 2016.

Controversy was Prince's first real foray into political songwriting, especially on the track 'Ronnie Talk to Russia', a plea to Ronald Reagan featuring the lyrics 'Ronnie if you're dead before I get to meet ya / Don't say I didn't warn ya' and 'Don't you blow up my world'.

Controversy re-entered the *Billboard* chart at number 55 after the singer's death.

Despite only reaching number 70 on the *Billboard* Hot 100 chart, 'Controversy' made it to number one on the *Billboard* Hot Dance Club Songs chart.

PARENTAL ADVISORY EXPLICIT CONTENT

C

IS FOR

CONTROVERSY

Prince pushed boundaries and courted controversy throughout his career, and *Controversy*, his fourth studio album, released in 1981, and the titular single, confronted his feelings about the public's reaction to his race, sexuality, gender and religion. Some of Prince's notoriously controversial moments included using the Lord's Prayer in the lyrics to 'Controversy' (which was considered blasphemous), singing about a sexual encounter with his sister at age 16 on the song 'Sister', and most famously, 'Darling Nikki', which openly referred to masturbation ('I knew a girl named Nikki, I guess you could say she was a sex fiend / I met her in a hotel lobby, masturbating with a magazine'), drawing the ire of Tipper Gore which reportedly led her to form the Parents Music Resource Centre (inventers of the Parental Advisory Stickers) after hearing her young daughter singing along to the song in 1984.

D IS FOR DISCOGRAPHY

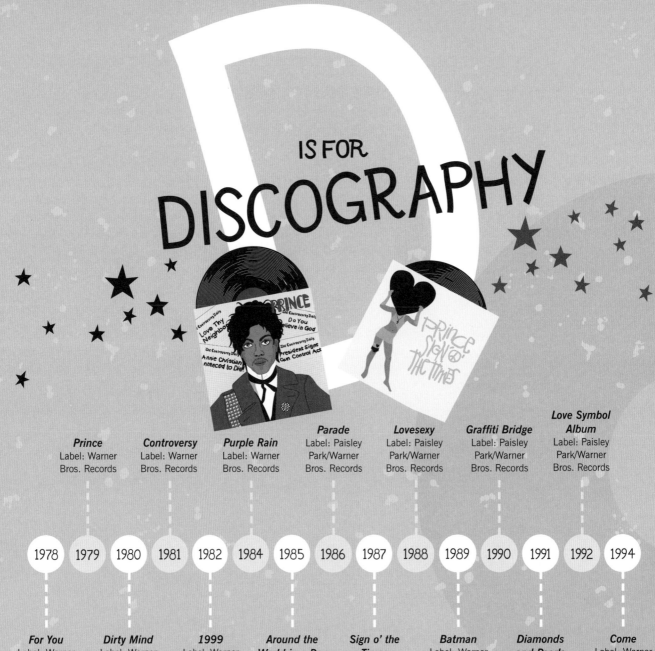

| | | | **Parade**
Label: Paisley
Park/Warner
Bros. Records | **Lovesexy**
Label: Paisley
Park/Warner
Bros. Records | **Graffiti Bridge**
Label: Paisley
Park/Warner
Bros. Records | **Love Symbol Album**
Label: Paisley
Park/Warner
Bros. Records |

Prince
Label: Warner
Bros. Records

Controversy
Label: Warner
Bros. Records

Purple Rain
Label: Warner
Bros. Records

1978 — 1979 — 1980 — 1981 — 1982 — 1984 — 1985 — 1986 — 1987 — 1988 — 1989 — 1990 — 1991 — 1992 — 1994

For You
Label: Warner
Bros. Records

Dirty Mind
Label: Warner
Bros. Records

1999
Label: Warner
Bros. Records

Around the World in a Day
Label: Paisley
Park/Warner
Bros. Records

Sign o' the Times
Label: Paisley
Park/Warner
Bros. Records

Batman
Label: Warner
Bros. Records

Diamonds and Pearls
Label: Paisley
Park/Warner
Bros. Records

Come
Label: Warner
Bros. Records

The Black Album
Label: Warner
Bros. Records

Prince was exceptionally prolific. He released 39 studio albums, four live albums, five soundtrack albums, 12 EP's, five compilations and 17 video albums – an extraordinary body of work. Surprisingly, this long list of releases only garnered three American number-one albums: *Purple Rain*, *Around the World in a Day* and, of all things, *Batman*. Prince was a ball of energy. As each project finished he wanted to move quickly onto the next one. This was at the root of his famous problems with his label Warner Bros. Records, who actually wanted him to slow down and take his time releasing records. Prince loathed this commercial control of his output. As a result, his discography features albums on different or multiple labels, sometimes within the same year. Famously, Prince still has many unreleased songs, locked away in a vault at Paisley Park. No doubt some of these recordings will see the light of day now that he has passed. We can only hope that those who have control over the contents of that vault now will be as discerning as Prince was in his lifetime.

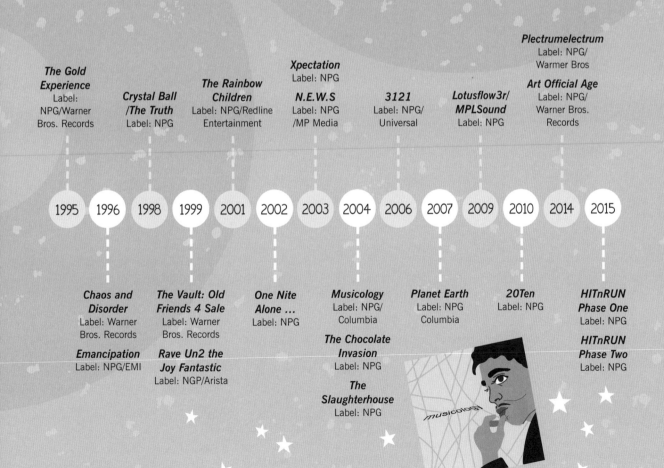

The Gold Experience
Label: NPG/Warner Bros. Records

Crystal Ball /The Truth
Label: NPG

The Rainbow Children
Label: NPG/Redline Entertainment

Xpectation
Label: NPG

N.E.W.S
Label: NPG /MP Media

3121
Label: NPG/ Universal

Lotusflow3r/ MPLSound
Label: NPG

Art Official Age
Label: NPG/ Warner Bros. Records

Plectrumelectrum
Label: NPG/ Warner Bros

1995 1996 1998 1999 2001 2002 2003 2004 2006 2007 2009 2010 2014 2015

Chaos and Disorder
Label: Warner Bros. Records

Emancipation
Label: NPG/EMI

The Vault: Old Friends 4 Sale
Label: Warner Bros. Records

Rave Un2 the Joy Fantastic
Label: NGP/Arista

One Nite Alone …
Label: NPG

Musicology
Label: NPG/ Columbia

The Chocolate Invasion
Label: NPG

The Slaughterhouse
Label: NPG

Planet Earth
Label: NPG Columbia

20Ten
Label: NPG

HITnRUN Phase One
Label: NPG

HITnRUN Phase Two
Label: NPG

musicology

E IS ALSO FOR

Emancipation

Prince's 19th studio LP came out in November 1996 on EMI music and his own imprint NPG records. The title was a direct reference to finally breaking away from his Warner Bros. Records contract. It's widely regarded as the first (non-compilation) R&B triple album ever released. The album's themes celebrate freedom and marriage (Prince had married Mayte Garcia that year), and a few tracks dealing with the death of their son Ahmir. Prince also experimented with genres and included covers for the first time (notably, a version of Joan Osborne's 'One of Us', where he pointedly changed the lyrics from 'Just a slob like one of us', to 'Just a slave like one of us').

...

'Emale'

Prince addressed the perils of modern technology in this track from *Emancipation*. The unusual track is more of a narrative, Prince seems to deal with a relationship gone wrong and the subsequent message of revenge left by email.

...

Ecstasy

Although unconfirmed, there's a well-documented story that Prince hallucinated one night after taking ecstasy, seeing the letters 'GOD' hovering over a field. This event was apparently the catalyst for the withdrawal of *The Black Album*. Prince apparently believed the album was too dark and subversive, and didn't want to corrupt his younger listeners.

...

'Extraordinary'

The only single to be released from Prince's 22nd studio album, *The Vault: Old Friends 4 Sale*, released in 1999. It became his sixth consecutive single to not make the *Billboard* chart.

On the original 12", 'Erotic City' featured a bracketed subtitle: 'Erotic City (Make Love Not War, Erotic City Come Alive)'.

WE CAN FUNK UNTIL THE DAWN...

The track also features in extended form on the B-side of the 1986 single 'Girls and Boys'.

Sheila E. denied that the song featured the word 'fuck', claiming that the line is 'We can funk until the dawn'. The subsequent (and somewhat disturbing) line 'Making love 'til cherry's gone' suggests otherwise. Other stand-out lyrics include 'If we cannot make babies, maybe we can make some time', 'I just want your creamy thighs / Baby, you're so creamy', and my favourite, 'All my purple life, I've been looking for a dame'.

A 2004 release was edited to cut out the possibly offensive lyric (see above) or to protect the public from 'mishearing' the lyric, so that radio stations could give it airplay without being fined.

When Prince inducted Parliament-Funkadelic into the Rock & Roll Hall of Fame he said the track was recorded right after seeing the group playing live in 1983 at the Los Angeles Beverly Theatre. In response George Clinton covered the song in the '94 film *PCU*.

E IS FOR EROTIC CITY

This B-side on the single 'Let's Go Crazy', 'Erotic City' has taken on a life of it's own over the years. Released in July 1984 (and again in 1986 and as an A-side in Germany in 1989) it quickly became one of the most requested Prince songs at live shows and in dance clubs. The low-slung groove and sleazy vocal, paired with the repeated high-key hook line make it cool and catchy in equal measure. The Parliament-Funkadelic influence is immediately apparent, with Prince's growled, half-spoken vocal mirroring George Clinton's style. The track was the first to feature singer and drummer Sheila E. on vocals alongside a Prince vocal that is both sped up and slowed down.

F

IS FOR

FASHION

No one wore it quite like Prince. He channelled everything from Beau Brummell's Regency-era foppishness to space-age pimp and flamboyant urban toreador – the diminutive Purple One proved that nothing was off limits. His gangster-chic Barbarella-meets-the-Godfather look was exactly that, he watched both films back to back and became inspired. He elevated the unpopular colour purple to stratospheric heights and, by championing high-waisted pants and Seinfeld-like puffy shirts, Prince was able to take some of fashion's biggest no-nos and turn them into a big 'yes, please'. A description of Prince's fashion tastes reads like a guide on 'what not to wear' – floral fingerless gloves, pink and white fur, Spanish ruffles, metallic stud shoulder pads, stripes, polka dots, flares and wide lapels – but whatever Prince wore, he wore oh-so very well. Prince's favourite designers included Armani, Gaultier and Lagerfeld, but mostly, he worked with a series of personal designers, including Cynthia Vargas Sieloff, Marie France and Stacia Lang, to create his signature looks.

Designer Stacia Lang worked with Prince for three years in the early 90s. She said, 'He never wears jeans and a T-shirt, but he has to be comfortable – lots of silks and crepes. By day, he sticks to tailored looks but at night he wants to look dramatic. He loves to reveal his physique with nipped-in waistlines. Hats add drama to an outfit.'

Following Prince's death, Frank Ocean published a tribute on his personal Tumblr, saying, 'He was a straight black man who played his first televised set in bikini bottoms and knee-high heeled boots, epic. He made me feel more comfortable with how I identify sexually simply by his display of freedom from and irreverence for obviously archaic ideas like gender conformity etc.'

Stacia Lang designed the infamous butt-baring outfit Prince wore to perform 'Gett Off' at the 1991 MTV Music Awards – although the eye-popping design feature was apparently his idea.

Prince not only worked with personal designers, he also employed a personal dresser and would not allow anyone else to dress him.

When Prince put on his yellow bolero and high-waisted onesie, with yellow shoes and matching guitar for a *Vogue* shoot, he reportedly said to the photographer, 'Tell me if this makes you want to puke.'

Prince had six separate costume ensembles on his *Diamonds and Pearls* tour.

Family
Prince was born Prince Rogers Nelson, the son of John Lewis Nelson and Mattie Della Shaw. Both of his parents were African American with a heritage based in Louisiana. Mattie was a jazz singer and John was a songwriter and piano player who performed in a jazz ensemble called the Prince Rogers Trio. Prince had one sister, Tyka Evene. Prince's parents separated when he was ten. John Nelson said he called his son Prince because he wanted him to do anything that he wanted to do.

...

Fentanyl
The drug that was ultimately believed responsible for Prince's death, Fentanyl is a painkiller that's estimated to be 80 times more potent than morphine and over one hundred times more potent than pure heroin. Often used as a palliative-care drug and anesthetic, Fentanyl has been responsible for hundreds of overdoses.

...

For You
Prince's first album, released in April 1978 when he was just 20 years old. It featured the singles 'Soft and Wet' and 'Just as Long as We're Together'. The album reached 163 on the *Billboard* chart. Prince wrote and played everything on the album with the exception of 'Soft and Wet', which he co-wrote with music producer and engineer Chris Moon.

...

'Funk Machine'
The first song Prince ever wrote, at the tender age of seven. Sadly no record of the song exists.

...

'FALLINLOVE2NITE'
Prince recorded this song with Zooey Deschanel. He was a big fan of her show *New Girl* and once told her it was the only thing he watched apart from the news.

Girlfriends

Prince had many girlfriends during his life, the best-known including Kim Basinger, Bria Valente, Apollonia, Sheila E., Carmen Electra, Heidi Mark, a hinted liaison with Susanna Hoffs from the Bangles, Sherilyn Fenn and even an unconfirmed fling with Madonna. His relationship with Susan Moonsie informed the song 'When Doves Cry'. His longest relationships were with former-fiance Susannah Melvoin, (thanks to her we have 'Nothing Compares 2 U'), and ex-wives Mayte Garcia and Manuela Testolini.

...

Mayte Garcia

Prince married Mayte Garcia, his back-up dancer and singer, on Valentine's Day in 1996. Prince was 37 and Mayte was 22. The devastating loss of their son took its toll and they divorced in 1999.

...

The Gold Experience

Prince's 17th studio album was entirely self-produced. Released in September 1995, it was seen as a return to form after a loss of popularity in the years after 1987's *Sign o' the Times*. The album featured the hit single 'The Most Beautiful Girl in the World', Prince's only ever UK number one, which was written for Mayte Garcia. Prince described the song 'Gold' as being 'The next Purple Rain.' *The Gold Experience* reached number six on the *Billboard* chart.

...

'Gett Off'

The lead single of 1991's *Diamonds and Pearls*, and Prince's 49th single release, 'Gett Off' reached number 26 on the *Billboard* chart and number one on the dance chart. The song was an evolution of three previous Prince tracks, 'Glam Slam', 'Love machine', and the remix of 'New Power Generation'.

The original white version of the famous Cloud guitar is seen at the end of the film *Purple Rain* (and on the cover of the 12"). The guitar was accidentally destroyed at a concert.

Prince's guitar playing often drew comparisons to Jimi Hendrix but Prince thought that it was obvious he sounded more like Santana. He said, 'Hendrix played more blues, Santana plays prettier.'

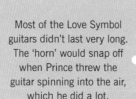

Most of the Love Symbol guitars didn't last very long. The 'horn' would snap off when Prince threw the guitar spinning into the air, which he did a lot.

Prince's Telecaster wasn't an original, he bought it early in his career. Hohner had brought the rights to Telecaster and reproduced this version, known as The Madcat. After a legal dispute, they stopped production making it a rare guitar. They produced two similar models later and appropriately named them The Prinz and the TE Prinz.

Prince had the Cloud guitars made in different coloured finishes – blue, peach, yellow, black and white.

In 2011, a Prince Fender Stratocaster with an entirely gold finish sold at a charity auction for US$100,000.

At one time it's said that he had four of the guitars which he named North, South, East and West. The Smithsonian has a white Cloud guitar on display. The yellow one sold at auction in 2016 for US$137,500.

G IS FOR GUITARS

Prince's iconic, superstar status, his instantly recognisable vocal style, over-the-top fashion and plethora of legendary sexy funk-pop singles often overshadows the fact that he was one of history's greatest guitar players. *Rolling Stone* ranked him number 33 in their top 100 guitarists, ahead of luminaries such as Muddy Waters, John Lee Hooker and Mick Ronson – no mean feat for someone who was better known for other things. His blistering lead break on 'Purple Rain' is legendary, probably the greatest lead break on a power ballad in history. He went full metal lead-line for 'When Doves Cry' and upstaged everyone at George Harrison's posthumous induction into the Hall of Fame in 2004, when he blew the roof off with his scorching solo on 'While My Guitar Gently Weeps'. Prince's favourite guitar was his Telecaster – it had a maple body and neck adorned with a leopard-print strap and pick guard. However, as with his clothing, he often preferred to have his own designs made up. Among his most memorable guitars were the purple and yellow 'Love Symbol' guitars originally made by Jerry Auerswald and the Cloud guitars built by Minneapolis makers Knut Koupee.

H IS FOR HEROES

Prince absorbed and blended a surprising range of artists. His mop of hair and flamboyant style instantly recalls Little Richard and Jerry Lee Lewis. Miles Davis, himself an influence, described Prince as a combination of James brown, Jimi Hendrix and Marvin Gaye – with a hint of Charlie Chaplin. On stage he was a hybrid with the hips of Elvis and the pout and strut of Mick Jagger, pushed over the top by his own high-energy acrobatics. He listened extensively to Joni Mitchell while growing up and cited David Bowie, Todd Rundgren and even Led Zeppelin as influences. George Clinton and Parliament-Funkadelic shaped many of his sounds and Carlos Santana was his guitar hero. Other musical loves included Sly Stone, Stevie Wonder and Curtis Mayfield, and he even liked the Beatles with the Sgt. Pepper influence all over his *Around the World in a Day* psychedelic period.

Prince never admitted that Elvis was an influence, but his manager Bob Cavallo once said, 'He wanted to be Elvis' when asked what Prince's dreams were. Prince performed both 'Jailhouse Rock', and 'All Shook Up' in his live shows.

In an interview with *New York Magazine,* Joni Mitchell said, 'Prince used to write me fan mail with all of the U's and hearts that way that he writes. And the office took it as mail from the lunatic fringe and just tossed it!'

In 1985, Prince described Joni Mitchell's 1975 album *The Hissing of Summer Lawns* as 'the last album I loved all the way through'.

Regarding the comparisons with Jimmy Hendrix, Prince once said, 'It's only because he's black. That's really the only thing we have in common.' Having said that, he covered 'All Along the Watchtower' at the Superbowl and stated that he didn't know much about Bob Dylan, but loved the Hendrix version of the song.

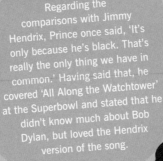

Prince once said, 'I saw critics be so critical of Stevie Wonder when he made *Journey Through the Secret Life of Plants*. Stevie has done so many great songs, and for people to say, "You missed", well … I would never say, "Stevie Wonder, you missed."

When asked about James Brown's influence on him in an interview for *The Telegraph*, Prince replied, 'That's a whole conversation! We haven't got time for that conversation.'

H IS ALSO FOR

Hair
Prince famously had his own hair salon. One of his personal hairdressers, Sherry Heart, recalled first time she cut his hair, 'I was shaking. I was doing the scissors over his ears and I had to hold my hand steady. I thought, "I'm cutting fucking Prince's hair!"' Among his most memorable hairstyles were the oversized afro, gelled curls, the Lovesexy flick, the Parade crop and 'The Tornado'.

…

Houses
Prince owned many properties, including his childhood home, the Minnesota weatherboard house his character 'The Kid' grew up in the film *Purple Rain* and of course his compound, Paisley Park. Prince also owned a house on Lake Riley in the early '80s, which he had painted purple, and following this he moved to the yellow house in Galpin, which had a built-in studio where he recorded *Sign o' the Times* and *The Black Album*.

HITnRUN Phase One and *Two*
Prince's final studio albums, his 38th and 39th respectively. Both were released on the streaming service Tidal before their physical realease through NPG records. *Phase One* reached number 48 on the *Billboard* chart, *Phase Two* reached number 40.

…

'How Come You Don't Call Me Anymore'
This B-side to the single '1999' featured on the soundtrack for the film *Girl 6*. It was covered by Alicia Keys.

…

'Head'
This track from *Dirty Mind* is one of Prince's most explicit. The tale of a bride-to-be and a chance encounter with a horny Prince … you can probably guess the rest.

I IS ALSO FOR

Instruments

Prince was an extremely talented multi-instrumentalist. He has been credited with playing around 27 instruments on his debut LP *For You*. Aside from the guitar (electric, bass and acoustic) he played piano, drums (bongos, congas, Syndrums), wind chimes and wood blocks. Among the lesser-known instruments he played were the water drum (a membrane over a water filled drum), the brush trap or 'guira' (a metal scraper-style instrument) and the bell tree.

...

The internet

Prince said in an interview with *The Mirror* in 2010, 'The internet's completely over. I don't see why I should give my new music to iTunes or anyone else. They won't pay me an advance for it and then they get angry when they can't get it.'

...

'I Could Never Take the Place of Your Man'

The fourth and final single from *Sign o' the Times*. One of Prince's poppiest singles, it featured an almost 'alternative' style keyboard and guitar line, unusual for Prince.

...

'I Would Die 4 You'

The fourth single from *Purple Rain*, 'I Would Die 4 You' reached number 8 on the *Billboard* chart when it was released, and reached number 39 after Prince's death. A 31 minute version of the in-studio jam featuring The Revolution and Sheila E. was released as a bootleg.

...

Instagram

Prince had his own instagram account called, of course, Princestagram. His last post was a white square, three days before his death.

When asked if he ever paid attention to the things that were written about him Prince replied, 'Only the parts that say I'm insane. I find that really humorous.'

NEXT QUESTION...

Chris Rock told *Vanity Fair* that the reason he got a good interview out of Prince was because everybody else tiptoed around him. 'I'm the only one who had the balls to ask Prince the tough questions!'

I DON'T TALK ABOUT THE PAST...

Mel B asked Prince why he chose her to interview him, he replied, 'Because you're a pimp. Look at this watch.'

In his last interview (for *Rolling Stone*), Prince dissed Justin Bieber, saying he had 'no personality'.

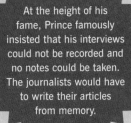

At the height of his fame, Prince famously insisted that his interviews could not be recorded and no notes could be taken. The journalists would have to write their articles from memory.

One of the few times Prince really opened up in an interview was when avid fan Chris Rock spoke to him in 1997. Among his revelations were that when his mother remarried, she taught him about 'the birds and the bees' by giving him *Playboy* magazines.

IS FOR

INTERVIEWS

Prince was well known for being a difficult person to interview. He always seemed to come across as polite and quietly spoken, but extremely hesitant to give anything of himself away, repeatedly referring to how 'normal' he was and how little mystery surrounded him. Of course, this only served to increase the mystique. Questions about a rivalry with Michael Jackson were frequently met with the response, 'next question'; questions about his current love life were met with, 'self-interest is on the back-burner now'; and questions about his childhood were met with, 'I don't talk about the past'. He was quiet and guarded and yet, there are still a few great Prince interviews on film, even if they give only a glimpse into how funny and engaging he could be. Interviews of note include an appearance on *The Oprah Winfrey Show* in 1996, a 1997 BBC interview that shows Prince in fine form alongside one of his heroes Larry Graham, bass player for Sly and the Family Stone, and an interview done by Mel B of the Spice Girls at Paisley Park in 1998. Prince's last talk-show appearance was on *The Arsenio Hall Show* in 2014 and his final recorded interview was with *Rolling Stone*.

Prince was raised as a Seventh-day Adventist, both his parents were strict devotees of the faith. He became a Jehovah's Witness in 2003 when he was introduced to the religion by Sly and the Family Stone bass player Larry Graham. Prince said, 'The more he said, the more I realised the truth.' By the end of 2001, Prince had stopped swearing and cut quite a few songs from his live sets that he thought were overtly raunchy. *Rolling Stone* referred to him in one article as 'The Freak in the Pulpit'. Prince explained his interest in religion as way to explain many of the injustices he witnessed. He said, 'I'm very practical. You go Trekkie on me, I got to go.' In 2004 he said faith and the Bible helped him with his music and all aspects of life, 'Once you can clean out the cobwebs, so to speak, you can see everything more clearly.' He attended church at Kingdom Hall of Jehovah's Witnesses in Minnetonka, Minnesota where he was known as Brother Nelson. He was described by churchgoers as quiet but very involved in group discussions and door knocking. The church held a memorial service for him when he died, attended by Larry Graham, Sheila E. and Sinbad.

J IS FOR JEHOVAH'S WITNESS

DEATH WILL BE NO MORE...

When he died, many people thought that Prince had refused medical treatment because of his religion.

One of Prince's favorite bible passages was Revelations 21:3-4, which says that in the end, Jehovah will live with his people and 'death will be no more'.

Sheila E. told *Billboard*, 'When I first met him he believed in God, but after that there was a time when it seemed like he didn't believe in anything … But then he became a Witness, and I felt, for him, that believing in something was better than nothing.'

Prince would often go door to door, evangelising for the faith. He said, 'Sometimes people act surprised. But mostly they're really cool.' Sheila E. said, 'It helped him with communicating with people more, reaching out and being connected … It opened him up to the world.'

When The Revolutions founding member Wendy Melvoin suggested a tour in 2000, Prince told her she would have to give a press conference denouncing her homosexuality and converting from Judaism to Jehovah for the tour to go ahead. She refused, and Prince eventually agreed to the tour.

Prince openly declared that, as a Jehovah's Witness, he was against gay marriage, which distressed many of his fans.

J

IS ALSO FOR

Michael Jackson

Prince and Michael Jackson were undisputed rivals. Jackson once described Prince as, 'One of the rudest people I've ever met,' and said that, 'Prince has always been a meanie. He's just a big meanie.' Prince refused to duet with Jackson on 'Bad', because he didn't want to share the limelight with anyone. Prince went out of his way to antagonise Jackson on several occasions. In a famous incident, Jackson turned up to the studio where Prince was polishing *Under the Cherry Moon*. Prince challenged him to a game of table tennis and then proceeded to thrash him, later saying, 'He played like Helen Keller.'

…

Janet Jackson

Prince had an ongoing feud with Janet Jackson. This was partly because he was fighting with Michael but it was allegedly also because Jimmy Jam and Lewis refused to give him the song, 'What Have You Done For Me Lately'. Apparently Prince loved the song and told them not to give it to Janet. They did, and as a result she signed the (at the time) biggest record deal in history – US$80 million with Virgin Records. Reports say he walked around Paisley Park saying 'fucking Janet Jackson' over and over.

…

Rick James

Prince supported sex funk supremo Rick James on his 1980 *Fire It Up* tour in what was ultimately seen as a changing of the funk guard. James was not a fan and told *Rolling Stone* '[Prince is a] a mentally disturbed young man. He's out to lunch. You can't take his music seriously. He sings songs about oral sex and incest.' He described Prince as a 'science-fiction creep' and said that onstage he wore a trench coat, which he took off to reveal 'little girl bloomers'. James also insisted that Prince was copying his moves.

K IS ALSO FOR

Chaka Kahn

Chaka Kahn had a worldwide hit with 'I Feel For You', a song Prince originally wrote for his self-titled LP in 1979. Kahn's single went to number one in the UK and number three on the *Billboard* chart in 1983. She named her 1984 album after the song and it featured such luminaries as Grand Master Flash and Stevie Wonder. After his death, Chaka Kahn called Prince her 'brother', and said she was honouring his memory by entering rehab for her addiction to Fentanyl, the same drug that killed Prince.

...

Kraftwerk

Prince performed at Coachella after Kraftwerk. He was added at the last minute. Portishead complained about the addition, as they were meant to be co-headlining. Prince is seen as an electronic music pioneer alongside Kraftwerk and Gary Numan, due to the minimalist funk he generated on synthesisers and his passionate love for the Linn Drum.

...

Kim Kardashian

Prince kicked Kardashian offstage at his *Welcome 2* tour in 2011. He spotted her in the front row and asked her onstage, but when he started gyrating around and she refused to join in, he lightheartedly said, 'Get off my stage'. Later Kardashian said, 'I was so nervous I froze when Prince touched me!'

...

Knees

Sheila E. stated that Prince had hip problems from dancing but that he also had problems with his knees, the result of performing in high heels, especially landing leaps from the stage stairs. She said, 'I mean, you think about all the years he was jumping off those risers. They were not low – they were very, very high – and to jump off that ... We did a year of touring [and] for him to jump off of that – just an entire year would have messed up his knees.'

In 1986, industrial-pop outfit Age of Chance took their punky dance cover of the song to number one on the UK Indie singles chart.

Experimental synth-pop group The Art of Noise covered the song in 1988. Tom Jones sung the vocal and the resulting single went to number five in the UK singles chart.

The music video was the first of several collaborations with fashion photographer Rebecca Blake, who had never really worked on a film project before.

Mazarati had just one hit in 1986 with the Prince-penned song '100 MPH'.

Rebecca Blake recalled to *The Golden Age of Music Video*, 'I was shooting Sheila E. and her band. And he rolled down the window of the limo slightly and had a good look at me while I was working and then just disappeared.' She received a call from his management a few weeks later, asking her to direct the 'Kiss' video.

Prince performed the song on *Ellen* in 2003 during the first season of the talk show. It was an unusual move for him to appear on a show before it had proved itself. Ellen produced her copy of his first album and Prince said, 'That's why I'm here – she's from the old school, she knows what's up.'

Julia Roberts belted out her own version in the film *Pretty Woman*.

K

IS FOR

KISS

Widely regarded as one of Prince's best songs – 'Kiss' heralded a new era for funk music. In an incredibly bold move, Prince dropped the bass right out of the track, creating a new style of minimalist funk that still influences people today. Warner Bros. Records were obviously freaked out by the lack of bass and didn't want to release it as a single. A last minute inclusion on *Parade*, 'Kiss' went on to be one of Prince's most memorable and successful tracks, packing dance floors in clubs all over the world – cue screaming, 'Act your age, not your shoes size!' *NME* ranked 'Kiss' number four in their 150 greatest songs of all time, and the best single of 1986. It reached number one on the *Billboard* chart, number six in the UK and number two in both Australia and New Zealand. Prince originally wrote the song for former The Revolution bassist Brownmark's band, Mazarati, who recorded it stripped-down with a sparse, funky bass. When Prince heard it, he was so impressed that he took the song back for himself and added the guitar parts. He left Mazarati's backing vocals as they were, pulled down the bass fader on the mixing desk and the rest, as they say, is history.

IS FOR

LOVE SYMBOL

In 1993, Prince famously changed his name to an unpronounceable glyph. He was in the middle of a dispute with Warner Bros. Records, and the change was a bold act of defiance. It seemed a little nutty at the time, and has been the butt of many a joke since, but Prince's act was not only highly original, it was dangerous, career-breaking and of course, brilliantly ahead of it's time. Prince's 14th studio album featured the glyph on the cover in place of both the title and the artist's name, and attempts to verbalise the glyph resulted in the album being commonly referred to as *Symbol* or *Love Symbol* (the glyph itself copyrighted as 'Love Symbol #2'). Despite the fact that no one knew what to call it, the album still reached number five on the *Billboard* chart, and hit number one in the UK, Australia and Austria. It was the last album to feature his backing band The New Power Generation. The symbol remained Prince's stage name until 2001, after his contract with Warner Bros. had finally expired.

At the time of creating the symbol, Prince already had plans for using the shape for a guitar and in designs for various stage sets.

Prince wanted the iconic glyph to represent gender fluidity. He also deliberately put it slightly off balance so that it was 'asymmetrical, like the human body.'

A floppy disc with a downloadable version of the glyph was sent out to media so that they could include it in their press coverage.

The press started referring to Prince as 'The Artist Formerly Known as Prince'

DAILY NEWS

THE ARTIST FORMERLY KNOWN AS

The symbol also contains a cross, and so becomes a true melding of Prince's two sides, sex and religion.

The Warner Bros. Records dispute was unusually due to the label wanting Prince to *slow down* his output. The symbol created a marketing nightmare as they couldn't say or even print his name.

The symbol was designed by Paisley Park's graphic designers Mitch Monson and Lizz Luce. Prince told them he wanted a fusion of the female 'Venus' and male 'Mars' symbols.

Live
Prince was known for his extraordinary live performances. He famously appeared after Michael Jackson onstage with James Brown, showing both performers up by whipping off his shirt and performing an improvised guitar solo and a guttural 'When Dove's Cry' scream.

...

'Little Red Corvette'
Released in 1983 as the first single from *1999*, 'Little Red Corvette' was Prince's biggest hit up to that point, and his first to rank higher on the pop charts than on the R&B chart. The song uses various automobile references as a metaphor for sex, with the Little Red Corvette in question being a short-term flame who Prince advises to slow down and find 'A lover who's gonna last.'

...

Lovesexy
Prince's 10th studio LP, released on May 10, 1988. Issued as a quick substitute following the cancellation of *The Black Album*, it was recorded in just seven weeks at Paisley Park. The cover features a nude Prince, which led to the album being wrapped in black by many record stores – ironic as it was replacing *The Black Album*.

...

'Let's Go Crazy'
A peppy number one hit single from 1984's *Purple Rain*. The track features two blistering guitar solos, parts of which Public Enemy sampled for 'Brother's Gonna Work It out.'

...

Like a Prayer
Prince played guitar on three tracks from Madonna's 1989 album *Like a Prayer*, 'Act of Contrition', 'Keep It Together' and the album's classic title track. The two also co-wrote 'Love Song,' which was recorded at Paisley Park Studios.

M

IS ALSO FOR

Manic Monday
Prince wrote this classic hit recorded by the Bangles in 1986. Unsubstantiated rumors circulated that Prince told Susanna Hoffs she could have the song if she slept with him. Hoffs has denied this, but stated that the song was responsible for their success as it set their career in motion. The songwriting credit is listed as 'Christopher'.

...

Morrissey
After Prince's death, Morrissey praised him saying, 'Prince is the royal people love. Prince has influenced the world more than is suspected, and somehow the life of his music is just beginning, and he would be thanked not only by humans but also animals for living his lyrical life as he did.'

...

Muppets
Prince appeared in a 1997 episode of *Muppet's Tonight*, singing the psychedelic 'Starfish and Coffee'. In the episode, various Muppets poke fun at him for his recent name change to 'the symbol', and Prince also sings 'Raspberry Sorbet' to the tune of 'Raspberry Beret'.

...

Movies
Prince made four movies in his lifetime: *Purple Rain*, *Under the Cherry Moon*, *Sign o' the Times* and *Graffiti Bridge*. *Purple Rain* was directed by Albert Magnoli and won Prince an Oscar for Original Song Score. Prince directed the other three films, with *Under the Cherry Moon* winning three Golden Raspberry Awards in 1986, tying with *Howard the Duck* for Worst Picture.

...

Chris Moon
Producer Chris Moon is credited with discovering Prince and cutting his first demo. Moon said that Prince was very shy when he first started recording. He said, 'He was singing. I could see his lips moving and I had my volumes turned all the way up, but I couldn't get the needles to move.'

After his death, Minnesotan locals set up a petition to make Prince's birthday, June 7, a public holiday, and to rename a terminal at Minneapolis–Saint Paul International Airport after him.

Before his death, Prince was often seen around Minneapolis, shopping at the local Walmart, browsing records at Electric Fetus or picking up his favourite wild-rice soup at Byerly's grocery store.

Days before his death, Prince dropped in to his favourite record store, Electric Fetus, and bought six CDs. According to Bob Fuchs, the store's retail music manager, the albums were Stevie Wonder's *Talking Book*, Chambers Brothers' *The Time Has Come*, Joni Mitchell's *Hejira*, Swan Silvertones' *Inspirational Gospel Classics*, Missing Persons' *The Best Of Missing Persons* and Santana's *Santana IV*.

Bob Dylan also came from Minneapolis, but once he left, he never returned.

GlamSlam

Other famous musical residents of Minneapolis include alternative acts The Replacements and Hüsker Dü (although they are technically from Saint Paul).

Prince owned a nightclub in Minneapolis called Glam Slam.

Prince's sound became its own genre, known as The Minneapolis Sound – a combination of funk rock, synth pop and new wave.

Prince loved Minneapolis – and Minneapolis loved him back. He will forever be linked to his beloved city as much as he's linked to the colour purple. Much of Prince's life and career is forever entwined with the city's culture. His music and lyrics reflect the place and in turn live on in the city's mythos. Prince was never far from home. He lived in and around Minneapolis for most of his life and most of his properties, including Paisley Park, were not far from the city centre. He was by far Minneapolis' most famous resident and regularly performed and attended shows at local venues Dakota Jazz Club and First Avenue, the latter being where the album version of 'Purple Rain' was recorded live and where scenes from the film were shot (as well as other Minneapolis locations such as Cedar Lake and the Orpheum Theater). He would regularly stage gigs at Paisley Park for locals and he even put on a performance for the Minnesota Lynx when they nabbed the WNBA championship in 2015.

IS FOR

MINNEAPOLIS

N

IS FOR
NOTHING
COMPARES 2 U

'Nothing Compares 2 U' was an instant hit for Sinead O'Conner and is still one of the songs most likely to roll a single tear down everyone's cheek. Powerful and anthemic, yet heart-wrenching and vulnerable, it's the go-to sing-along sad song for anyone who has loved and lost. Released in 1985 on the debut LP for Prince's side project The Family, the track remained relatively unknown until O'Conner released it in 1990 for her album *I Do Not Want What I Haven't Got* and took it to number one in the US and in 11 other countries around the world. Prince re-released his version of the song in 1993 on his triple-CD compilation album *The Hits/The B-Sides*. On the day of Prince's death, the Apollo Theatre in New York became the site of an impromptu gathering in his memory. The signage read, 'In honor of the beautiful one Prince, Nothing Compares 2 U 1958–2016'.

Soundgarden vocalist Chris Cornell recorded a version of the song, which he posted online after Prince died with the words, 'I pay tribute to this unequalled artist who has given all our lives so much inspiration.

When asked about Prince, O'Connor said, 'We didn't get along at all. In fact, we had a punch up … He told me he didn't like me saying bad words in my interviews, so I told him to fuck off. He got quite violent … He really packed a punch. Bigger than mine.' She also referred to him as 'a heel in heels'.

!?#%*@

+?#&?!^

Prince said of the Sinead O'Connor version of the song, 'I love it, it's great! I look for cosmic meaning in everything. I think we just took that song as far as we could, then someone else was supposed to come along and pick it up.'

In an interview on BBC Radio 6 Music, O'Conner said of the enduring quality of the song, 'It's really about emotions, it's not about notes … I never sing a song that I can't emotionally identify with.' She said the tear in the video is real – she was thinking about the death of her mother who died when O'Connor was 17. O'Conner was also very influenced by Bel Canto, an Italian school of singing where the emotional content of the words is reflected in the vocal tones and register.

'Nothing Compares 2 U' was written about Susannah Melvoin, sister of The Revolution guitarist Wendy Melvoin, who Prince was engaged to and had a long-standing relationship with.

N IS ALSO FOR

The New Power Generation

Also known as the NPG, The New Power Generation were the band Prince formed following the demise of The Revolution. The NPG were first mentioned in the opening track on *Lovesexy*, with Prince proclaiming, 'Welcome to the New Power Generation.' The song 'New Power Generation' appeared on the *Graffiti Bridge* soundtrack, and the band name was mentioned in the film. When Prince was in dispute with Warner Bros. Records he used the NPG as a side project so he could release material on other labels, although his presence was downplayed on the releases. The main NPG members played with Prince on the *Nude* tour in support of 1991's *Diamonds and Pearls*: drummer Michael Bland, keyboard player Tommy Barbarella, Levi Seacer Jnr on guitar, Sonny T on bass, and Rosie Gaines and Tony M on vocals. The NPG contributed to four Prince albums and released three under their own name. They re-united as Prince's backing band for his final album, *HITnRUN Phase Two*.

…

New Girl

Prince appeared in an episode in the third season of TV comedy *New Girl* starring Zooey Deschanel. The episode was simply called 'Prince' and revolves around the gang from the show going to a party at Prince's house. Apparently Prince was a huge fan of the show and contacted Deschanel directly asking to make an appearance.

…

'Nasty Girl'

Prince wrote this song for Vanity 6. It was released as their second single in September 1982. It reached number one on the *Billboard* Hot Dance Club chart and number 9 on the UK charts. Denise Matthews (Vanity) later denounced the song after becoming a Christian in 1994.

O
IS ALSO FOR

Orange

We can add yet another outrageous colour to Prince's signature purple and statement yellow. Prince wore a blazing orange jacket, pants and shirt at the press conference for the legendary Superbowl performance. He wore a shimmering orange outfit when he presented the award to Beck for best album at the 2015 MTV awards, (his look when Kanye pulled another 'Taylor Swift' moment when Beyonce didn't win the award is priceless). For his 1992 tour, Prince wore an orange jumpsuit with black piping and emblazoned with musical notes.

...

Orphans

Prince secretly donated to many charities, but he was particularly commited to working with a charity called PARSA, an organisation that helped to guide Afghan orphans away from the influence of extremist groups. Prince provided this money through HALO (Helping and Loving Orphans), a charity run by Seattle philanthropist Betty Tisdale.

...

Orgasm

Prince moved from the euphemistic 'Cream' in 1991 to just spelling it out with 'Orgasm' in 1994. An appropriate track to 'finish' the album *Come*, 'Orgasm' is basically a lot of whispered words and orgasm noises over guitar feedback and ocean sounds.

...

One Nite Alone

Prince's 25th studio album, released in May 2002 on NPG records. The record is what it says on the box: Prince solo, singing and playing piano. There is only minimal use of other instruments. Proving his lifelong devotion to Joni Mitchell he covers her song 'A Case Of You' and thanks her in the liner notes. The album was released online only and has never been available instore. The credits include Prince's doves Divinity and Majesty as providing ambient noise.

MY FRIEND THE ARTIST

Unsure what to call Prince since he had changed his name to the symbol, Oprah referred to him throughout the interview as, 'my friend the artist'.

Mayte later said about the appearance, and not mentioning the death of their son, 'We believed he was going to come back, that souls come back. We didn't want to acknowledge he was gone, it was our way of grieving.'

Oprah said that because Prince was in touch with his masculine and feminine side, 'People grew up thinking that you were weird or that you were gay. That never bothered you?' Prince replied, 'Whatever floats the boat.'

Prince said in the interview that he wanted his legacy to be his music.

Prince told Oprah he had one song a day inside himself until the day he died.

IS FOR

OPRAH

Prince appeared on *The Oprah Winfrey Show* in 1996, in one of his few, and most famous interviews. It was his first media appearance after changing his name to an unpronounceable symbol. Wearing an oversized white knit jumper, Prince took Oprah on a tour through Paisley Park and played her a snippet of 'Purple Rain' on the piano. Prince's then wife Mayte Garcia was also interviewed and appears to be clearly enamoured with Prince, who is much more reserved. The interview took place just a week after the couple tragically lost their newborn son Ahmir Gregory Nelson, who was born with Pfeiffer syndrome, a genetic disorder. Clearly still coming to terms with their grief, Prince and Mayte proceeded with the interview as though nothing had happened, even giving Oprah a tour of the baby's room. There had been rumours about the health of their baby, so Oprah inquired, 'What is the status of your baby, your pregnancy, your…' To which Prince heartbreakingly replied, 'Well, our family exists… We're just beginning it. We've got many kids to have, a long way to go.'

P IS FOR PURPLE RAIN

Talk about your iconic 80's images: the purple Prince astride his purple motorbike, sporting frilled sleeves and a high collar in a smoke-filled alley. You can't look at it without wanting to belt out a few bars of the title track. 'Purple Rain' the song is easily one of the world's most enduring, anthemic ballads. *Purple Rain* the album was Prince's sixth, released in June 1984 as a soundtrack to the film of the same name, a quasi-autobiographical drama with Prince playing the troubled frontman of The Revolution, who uses music to escape his abusive family life. It's the sixth best-selling soundtrack of all time, is widely considered to be Prince's best album and it regularly pops up on 'best album ever' lists. It was number one on the *Billboard* chart for 24 weeks (re-entering at number two after Prince's death). It spawned two number one singles, 'Lets Go Crazy' and 'When Doves Cry'; the title track reached number two and 'I Would Die 4 U' made the top 10. The film was a hit, grossing US $68 million at the box office.

Purple Rain won Oscars for Best Original Music and Best Original Song Score, Grammys for Best Rock Performance and Best Score Soundtrack as well as a Hall of Fame Award in 2011.

'Purple Rain' was the last song Prince ever sang in concert.

The film's success and popularity is largely attributed to the music and the charisma (if not acting talent) of its leading man. The movie earned two Razzie Awards, one for Worst New Star, for Apollonia's performance, and one for Worst Original Song, for 'Sex Shooter'.

'I Would Die 4 U', 'Baby I'm a Star' and 'Purple Rain' were all recorded live at Minneapolis club First Avenue, with overdubs added later.

The album swapped the number one spot twice with Bruce Springsteen's *Born in the USA*.

Prince accepted his Academy Award wearing a sparkling purple-sequined hooded cape and flanked by a towering Wendy and Lisa. He thanked the Academy, his team and, 'most of all, God'.

The part played by Apollonia was originally written for Vanity of Vanity 6. Before Apollonia was cast, it was offered to *Flashdance* star Jennifer Beals, but she declined the role so she could attend college.

P
IS ALSO FOR

Paisley Park
Prince started his own record label, Paisley Park, in 1985. It was named after a song from the album *Around the World in a Day*. Prince's Paisley Park complex in Chanhassen, Minnesota, housed the label, recording studios, rehearsal spaces and an apartment. When the label ended in 1994, Prince continued to live and work at the compound. Following his death the complex is being turned into a museum.

...

Pseudonyms
Prince's most infamous pseudonym was definitely that unpronounceable symbol, however it was just one of many: he also referred to himself as Camille (when singing as a female) and he rarely used his own name when writing songs for other people, variously going by Jamie Starr, The Starr Company, Alexander Nevermind, Christopher and Joey Coco. When Prince was a child his nickname was Skipper, and throughout his career he was referred to as The Purple One, Love Symbol, The Artist, The Artist Formerly Known as Prince and TAFKAP. And when he changed his name back to Prince: The Artist Formerly Known as The Artist Formerly Known as Prince.

...

Purple
From the purple jacket on the cover of *Controversy* and *Purple Rain* onwards, purple was emblematic for Prince, not just in clothing, but stage sets, lighting and artwork. Of course it's the colour most associated with royalty, so it was perfect for someone called Prince. Purple also seemed to have a religious significance for Prince, who once said, 'When there's blood in the sky – red and blue [equals] purple ... purple rain pertains to the end of the world and being with the one you love and letting your faith/god guide you through the purple rain.' Prince's beloved NFL team was the Minnesota Vikings. The colour of their jersey? Purple.

Q IS ALSO FOR

Quotes

On people's opinions of him: 'I don't really care so much what people say about me because it usually is a reflection of who they are. For example, if people wish I would sound like I used to sound, then it says more about them than it does me.' On being cool: 'Cool means being able to hang with yourself. All you have to ask yourself is "Is there anybody I'm afraid of? Is there anybody who if I walked into a room and saw, I'd get nervous?" If not, then you're cool.' On philosophy: 'There's always a rainbow at the end of every rain.' On the world: 'It's a hurtful place, the world, in and of itself. We don't need to add to it. And we're in a place now where we all need one another, and it's going to get rougher.' On fame: 'Sometimes it takes years for a person to become an overnight success.' Ouch: 'Michael Jackson's album was only called Bad because there wasn't enough room on the sleeve for Pathetic.' Umm: 'Time is a mind construct. It's not real.'

...

Questlove

Percussionist and The Roots frontman Questlove was obsessed with Prince growing up. Later in life he got to hang out with Prince and even went rollerblading with him. He recalled one instance where the devout Prince made him put $20 in the curse jar for saying 'shit'. Questlove said, 'Hey, you taught me how to curse when I was little.'

...

'Q.U.E.E.N'

By 2013 Prince was regularly remixing tracks at Paisley Park with the help of youthful engineer Josh Welton. One of the few remixes to see the light of day was the track 'Q.U.E.E.N' by Janelle Monáe and Erykah Badu. Prince added a disco funk groove to the original track.

As Michael Jackson's producer, Quincy Jones was front and centre on the feud between Jackson and Prince. Quincy recounted that, following the infamous gig where Prince joined James Brown and Jackson on stage and, in Quincy's opinion, ended up making a fool of himself, Prince waited for Jackson and his crew after the show and attempted to run over them with his limo.

Quincy has stated that Prince said he was too shy to perform in front of other musicians, something that didn't stop the notoriously shy Michael Jackson.

Prince did end up contributing a song to the charity album: '4 the Tears in Your Eyes'.

Quincy was brought in to broker a meeting between Jackson and Prince, and he recalls that Prince turned up with a box full of random props from 'Under a Cherry Moon' (which Jackson thought Prince was using as voodoo), and Prince kept calling Jackson 'Camille.'

After Prince died Quincy tweeted 'RIP to @prince... a true artist in every sense of the word. Gone way too soon.'

Wendy Melvoin told Alan Light that the reason Prince didn't want to sing on 'We Are the World' was, in fact, because, 'He felt like the song was horrible.'

QUINCY JONES

Also known as Q, Quincy Jones is an American record producer who, in 1985, had been called in to co-produce the 'We Are the World' charity song – a project intended to raise money to combat starvation in Africa, especially Ethiopia. Susan Rogers, Prince's engineer at the time, told journalist Alan Light that she recalled the moment that Quincy called Prince to ask him to participate in the project. Prince declined but asked if he could play guitar on the track instead – apparently the answer was 'no', so he sent Sheila E. instead. Quincy again tried to coax Prince into performing for the charity single at the American Music Awards, but Prince's manager Bob Cavallo relayed Quincy that, once again, the only thing Prince would do was play guitar. Quincy apparently got quite angry, responding with, 'I don't need him to fucking play guitar!' Prince's absence from the song, followed by an altercation at a nightclub later that night, ended up generating a lot of bad press, as well as damaging his reputation among his peers.

R

IS FOR

RASPBERRY BERET

Maybe you work for Mr. Magee or you're a bit too leisurely? Maybe you walk in through the out door, or mix with the clouds on an overcast day? Either way, chances are you're into a raspberry beret. The song is about a first sexual encounter, whether it was Prince's or not is unclear, but the track embodies Prince's knack for writing about empowered female sexuality. 'Raspberry Beret' captures a kind of doe-eyed nostalgia – sure, it's about sex, but it's a fairly innocent outing compared to previous Prince tracks like 'Soft and Wet' and 'Dirty Mind'. 'Raspberry Beret' was originally recorded in 1982, but the classic was reworked with a more 'international' sound as a single for 1985's *Around the World in a Day*. The song is testament to the fact that Prince, the King of Funk, had no trouble writing a killer pop song.

The song featured on the soundtrack for Spike Lee's 1996 film *Girl 6*.

Pat Smear, founding member of the Foo Fighters and touring Nirvana guitarist, appeared in the video.

Liverpool's famed producer Ian Broudie took the name of his band The Lightening Seeds from a mishearing of the lyric: 'Thunder drowns out what the lightning sees.'

After Prince passed away, the song re-entered the *Billboard* chart at number 33. On release it reached number two, beaten to the number one spot by Duran Duran's 'A View to a Kill'. It only reached number 25 in the UK.

The 1985 recording of the song features the best-known line-up for Prince's famed backing band, The Revolution. Keyboardist Lisa Coleman was responsible for the string section.

Prince played cello on the track.

R IS ALSO FOR

The Revolution
Formed in 1979 and lasting until 1986, Prince's backing band saw a few changes, but the essential line-up is usually regarded as Lisa Coleman on keyboards and Wendy Melvoin on guitar (aka Wendy & Lisa), Bobby Z. on drums, Brown Mark on bass and Matt 'Doctor' Fink on keyboards. Along the way the line-up also included Dez Dickerson on guitar, Gayle Chapman on keyboards and Andre Cymone on bass. The final incarnation of the band in '85–86 featured Miko Weaver on guitar and Susannah Melvoin on backing vocals, with Eric Leeds on saxophone and Matt 'Atlanta Bliss' Blistan on trumpet. Wendy apparently said of her twin sister Susannah who joined the band, 'I shared a womb with this person, do I also have to share the stage?' Prince rehearsed the band under the name The Rebel.

...

The Rainbow Children
Prince's 24th studio album and the first under the name Prince after his time using the unpronounceable glyph as his moniker. The album also marked a return to more acoustic instruments, including live drums and horns. It was also the first album since Prince's conversion to a Jehovah's Witness, which is referred to in the lyrics as well as other aspects of religion, racism and sexuality. It is essentially a concept album, about a utopian society inspired by Martin Luther King.

...

'Red House'
Prince covered this song on the album *Power of Soul: A Tribute to Jimi Hendrix,* but, of course, he renamed it 'Purple House.'

S IS ALSO FOR

Sheila E.

Prince first encountered long-time friend and collaborator Sheila Escovedo in 1978, performing with her father, percussionist Pete Escovedo. After the show, Prince reportedly told her that he was fighting with his bass player over who got to be her husband. He vowed that she would be part of his band, but they didn't work together until *Purple Rain* in 1984. They had a brief romantic relationship and were engaged for a short time. Sheila E. had two solo chart hits with the Prince-penned singles 'Glamorous Life' and 'Love Bizarre'. She was drummer and percussionist for the New Power Generation, appearing on *Sign o' the Times* and *Lovesexy,* and her percussion solo on 'One Nite Alone...' is legendary. Devastated by Prince's death, she said, 'I couldn't look at a picture of him; I couldn't listen to his music.'

...

Super Bowl XLI

Prince nearly upstaged the game during his iconic 2007 halftime show, which beamed out to 140 million viewers. He played 'Let's Go Crazy', 'Baby I'm a Star', Queen's 'We Will Rock You', Credence Clearwater Revival's 'Proud Mary', The Foo Fighters' 'Best of You' and Bob Dylan's 'All Along the Watchtower', before finishing with a now legendary, epic version of 'Purple Rain', performed during a fortuitously-timed downpour.

...

Stalker

A woman used to appear on the swings at Paisley Park. Prince apparently approached her and said, 'Hey, all my friends in there say you're a stalker. And that I should call the police. But I don't want to do that, so why don't you tell me what you want to happen. Why are you here? How do you want this to end?' Prince said that after this she left and didn't come back, adding, 'All she wanted was to be seen.'

Rolling Stone writer Michaelangelo Matos called *Sign o' the Times* the 'last classic R&B album prior to hip hop's takeover of black music,' and, 'The final four-sided block-buster of the vinyl era.'

Prince originally pulled material from two abandoned projects *Camille* (where his vocals were sped up to resemble a female voice) and *Dream Factory,* an album featuring The Revolution. With added tracks Prince made a triple album set which he was going to release under the name *Crystal Ball.* Warner Bros. Records talked Prince into releasing it as a double LP instead.

Four tracks on *Sign o' the Times* feature Prince's female alter-ego Camille's vocals 'Housequake', 'Strange Relationship', 'U Got the Look' and 'If I Was Your Girlfriend'.

Prince credits engineer Susan Rogers as his strongest musical influence on the album, as it features very little input from other musicians and relied heavily on programming of the LinnDrum drum machine.

PRINCE SIGN 'O' THE TIMES

Time Out "GREATEST ALBUM OF ALL TIME"

The single 'Sign o' the Times' is viewed as Prince's equivalent to Grandmaster Flash's hit single 'The Message'.

In 1989 *Time Out* called *Sign o' the Times* the 'Greatest album of all time'.

SIGN O' THE TIMES

S IS FOR

Prince's ninth album, jointly released in March 1987 on Paisley Park and Warner Bros. Records, *Sign o' the Times* was the first album Prince released since breaking up The Revolution. A follow up to the hugely successful *Parade*, *Sign o' the Times* was originally intended to be a triple album, but was eventually whittled down to a double. It features the title track, a massive hit for Prince that reached number three on the *Billboard* chart and number one on the R&B chart. The album also features enduring Prince favourites 'U Got the Look', 'If I Was Your Girlfriend', and 'I Could Never Take the Place of Your Man'. The album remains one of his most critically acclaimed. It reached number six on the *Billboard* chart, went to number one in Switzerland and was certified platinum in the UK and USA.

T IS FOR

21 NIGHTS

In May 2007, Prince made the unprecedented announcement that he was going to play 21 concerts at The O2 Arena in Greenwich, which had recently risen from the ashes of the Millennium Dome. The event was part of *The Earth* tour and ran through most of August and select nights in September. Prince played most nights for 2–3 hours and hosted after parties that went into the early morning. Every night sold out and *The Telegraph* sent a guest to cover each performance, with reviewers including Sophie Ellis-Bextor, Bill Oddie and Jo Brand. The event was captured in Prince's book *21 Nights*, which features a lavish photo essay by Randee St Nicholas for each performance. The book was released with Indigo Nights, a CD/DVD exclusive which featured live footage from the shows, plus coverage of after parties and press conferences. Extras also included previously unseen images of Prince by Randee St Nicholas and a volume of Prince's poetry and lyrics.

As promo for the tour, Prince released his new album *Planet Earth* for free with the *Daily Mail*. It was the newspaper's highest selling edition since the death of Princess Diana.

At the time of the concerts, Prince said it would the last time he would play any of his hits – but he later reneged on that statement.

At one point during a performance, Prince wagged his finger at the audience and whispered, 'Foreplay starts in the mind.'

Michael Jackson tried to trump Prince two years later by announcing his own run of 50 concerts at The O2 Arena. He died before he could start the tour.

The Telegraph satirist Michael Deacon described the gig as a 'musical Christmas pudding', and called it 'too rich.' Sophie Ellis-Bextor wrote, 'He plays lots of songs you don't know.' Cellist Julian Lloyd Webber wrote that Prince reminded him me of a latter-day Cliff Richard, 'A great entertainer, and there's nothing wrong with that.' Jo Brand reported, 'The show was amazing, Prince himself an impressive multi-tasker and the experience something that will sit in my deteriorating memory for some time to come. I still don't like him, though.'

T

IS ALSO FOR

Tribute Concert
The official tribute concert for Prince was held at the Xcel Energy Center in Saint Paul on October 13th, 2016. Among the performers were Stevie Wonder and Chaka Kahn, with The New Power Generation, led by Morris Day, and members of 3rdeyegirl performing all the songs. The concert was topped off by a video message from President Barack Obama, thanking Prince for all he'd done, saying, 'You'll be in our hearts forever.'

...

'Thieves in the Temple'
Taken from the 1990 soundtrack to the film *Graffiti Bridge*, this single was released in July of that year. The song was a last-minute inclusion, and the final song recorded for the album – yet it went on to reach number one on the US R&B chart in September. Eddie Murphy and Michael Jackson sampled Prince's scream at the end for their duet 'Whatzupwitu'.

...

The Truth
Released as part of the *Crystal Ball* box set, which included three discs of previously bootlegged material, making up *Crystal Ball*, Prince's 20th studio album, and a fourth disc, *The Truth*, Prince's 21st studio album, which featured 12 acoustic tracks. The set was initially only available by mail order and also came with a limited-edition instrumental album xxxxxxby The NPG called *Kamasutra*.

...

20Ten
Prince's 35th studio album released in July, 2010 (hence the name). The album was released as a giveaway with the *Daily Mirror* and the *Daily Record* in the UK and through *Rolling Stone* in Germany and *Courrier International* in France. Describing the album as a personal diary of 2010, Prince recorded everything on the album except for backing vocals and horns. *20Ten* was never officially released in the US.

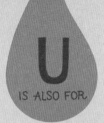

U

IS ALSO FOR

'U Got the Look'

The highest charting single from *Sign o' the Times*, 'U Got the Look', reached number two on the *Billboard* chart and appears on the Rock & Roll Hall of Fame's '500 Songs that Shaped Rock and Roll' list. Sheena Easton is not credited on the track, but she shares the lead vocal with Prince.

...

'Uptown'

The lead single from Prince's third album, *Dirty Mind,* released in September, 1980. The song is notable for being one of Prince's first forays into political funk, reimagining uptown Minneapolis as a utopian society where people can express their creativity free of prejudice. It features the lyrics: 'Baby didn't say too much / She said, "Are you gay?" / Kinda took me by surprise, I didn't know what to do / I just looked her in her eyes and I said, "No, are you?"'

...

Underwear

Guitarist Dez Dickerson recalled to the *Star Tribune* how, between shows at The Roxy in LA, Prince's manager Bob Cavallo would come to the dressing room with a list of critiques. He complained to Prince, 'You're wearing these Spandex pants with no underwear. It's obscene.' Dickerson said, 'When Bob left, Prince got that look on his face. He said, "Bob wanted me to wear underwear, so I'll wear underwear." So he went out in his underwear. Period.'

...

U

Prince frequently used the letter 'U' in place of the word 'you'. Always ahead of his time, he regularly used what are now familiar abbreviations in song titles such as 'U Got The Look', and 'Nothing Compares 2 U', and in his written correspondence.

Prince's character in the film was called 'Christopher Tracy', a name he later used as a pseudonym when writing songs for other musicians.

Melancholy ballad 'Sometimes it Snows in April', remained in Prince's live sets right up until his last performance.

Under the Cherry Moon was Kristin Scott Thomas' feature film debut.

Under the Cherry Moon was filmed in colour but shown in black and white.

Prince called in jazz arranger Clare Fischer to score the film, but removed most of the orchestration from the album *Parade*.

The film garnered five Razzie Awards, including tying with *Howard the Duck* for Worst Picture. Prince also picked up awards for Worst Actor and Worst Director.

Prince co-wrote the songs 'Under the Cherry Moon' and 'Christopher Tracy's Parade' with his father, John.

Mary Lambert (director of *Pet Sematary* and Madonna's infamous 'Like a Prayer' video) was originally set to direct the film, but was fired by Prince.

U IS FOR UNDER THE CHERRY MOON

The film *Under the Cherry Moon*, released in 1986, was Prince's directorial debut and his second feature as an actor. He starred alongside Kristin Scott Thomas in a musical drama about a gigolo swindler who falls in love with one of his targets. Reviews of the film were largely negative with many critics referring to it as a vanity project. Despite this, *Parade*, which was essentially the soundtrack album for the film, is considered one of Prince's best albums. Released in March 1986, *Parade* was Prince's eighth studio album and the last to feature The Revolution. It reached number three on the *Billboard* chart and featured one of Prince's most beloved hit singles, 'Kiss', which was a number one hit in America.

V IS FOR VAULT

In the basement of Prince's Minneapolis studio complex Paisley Park, accessible only by elevator, with a thick, steel, bank-style door complete with time lock and spinning wheel, openable only with a combination that only Prince knew, sits the vault – home to all unreleased Prince recordings. Thousands of hours of music lie in the vault. Prince would dip in every now and then, but many undiscovered songs remained. When Prince died he left no will, so Bremer Trust, the guardians of his estate, had to drill into the vault to see if it contained any last wishes and to create a full inventory of the things he left behind. What they found was an extensive range of unreleased material, along with assorted props and keepsakes. Prince himself said in an MTV interview in 1990, 'If U went in the vault U'd hear the REALLY erotic Prince.'

Two shelved promotional ideas: a cookbook with Martika called *Martika's Kitchen*, and an ice cream called 'Mr Freeze'.

The vault contained a complete replica of the Michael Keaton-era batsuit.

A script was found for *Under the Apple Tree*, a proposed sequel to *Under the Cherry Moon*.

Four BMX motorcross bicycles were found in the vault, all painted purple.

More than 3000 recordings were found in the vault, including *Sexy Drummrfunkr*, a collection of Shiela E. drum solos; Prince and the Revolution's *Dream Factory*, an unreleased double album from 1982; 1985's *The Rebels*, a rock album recorded with The Time; and an unnamed duets project with Stevie Nicks.

An EP was found featuring collaborations with Kim Basinger, Ween and Ozzy Osborne.

The original recordings were found for *The Flesh*, a project of live jam sessions including 'Junk Music' and 'The Undertaker', two often bootlegged Prince releases.

A hard rock record made with Bob Mould called *Bockwinkle* was in the vault.

There were two boxes of letters containing correspondence between Prince and Sinead O'Connor.

Aside from purple and yellow, Prince also seemed to have a thing for the colour teal. The vault held a copy of a recording called 'Teal', a 19-minute music video directed by Tim Burton called *Teal Snow* and a teal backdrop and six teal angel costumes for a stage show.

V IS ALSO FOR

Vegetarian
While Prince flirted with veganism – he described himself as a 'complete vegan' in 1997 – he reportedly loved cookies with milk and honey too much to give them up. He was, however, a lifelong vegetarian, and an active supporter of animal rights groups. He refused to wear wool and leather and never ate cheese. When asked why he was a vegetarian he said that he wouldn't 'eat anything with parents'.

...

Vanity 6
In 1981 Prince wanted to put together an act for his then girlfriend Susan Moonsie. He added Brenda Bennet and Jamie Shoop, who was then dropped in favour of Denise Matthews as the lead singer. Prince originally wanted to call the band, 'The Hookers', and for Matthews' name to be 'Vagina', pronounced Vagee-nah. Matthews disagreed, and reportedly christened herself Vanity. Prince said that looking at her was like looking at a female version of himself – so the name was appropriate. He added the '6' denoting the number of breasts in the band. Vanity 6 had a hit with 'Nasty Girl' in 1982 which went to number one on the *Billboard* Hot 100. The self-titled debut album went gold, but with Matthews abruptly leaving the group in 1983, it was also their last.

...

The Vault: Old Friends 4 Sale
Prince's 22nd studio album was released in September 1999, and was his last album released within his Warner Bros. Records contract. The material was taken from 1985–1994 and given to Warner Music in 1996 but remained unreleased for three years. The only single released from it was 'Extraordinary', and there was no accompanying tour to promote it. The record only reached 85 on the *Billboard* chart, pretty poor by Prince's standards.

W

IS ALSO FOR

'While My Guitar Gently Weeps'

Prince and George Harrison were inducted into the Rock & Roll Hall of Fame in 2004. To commemorate, Tom Petty, Jeff Lynne, Steve Winwood, George Harrison's son Dhani and Prince performed a version of 'While My Guitar Gently Weeps' at the Astoria Hotel. The performance is now legendary for Prince's scorching guitar solo – as well as his gravity-defying guitar toss at the end. Drummer Steve Ferrone said, 'I just saw it go up, and I was astonished that it didn't come back down again. Everybody wonders where that guitar went, and I gotta tell you, I was on the stage, and I wonder where it went, too.'

...

Wedding

Prince and Mayte Garcia had an extravagant wedding on Valentine's Day in 1996. Mayte wore a white gown and a gold pendant shaped like Prince's love symbol. When they said their 'I dos', white doves were released into the sky. The chinaware at the reception was emblazoned with the love symbol with an 'M' in the centre.

...

Wealth

Prince's net worth is estimated at around US $300 million.

...

'When You Were Mine'

A song from *Dirty Mind*, 'When You Were mine' wasn't released as a single but gained popularity on the promotional release for the album, which also contained the soon-to-be single, 'Uptown'. 'When You Were Mine' proved so popular that it made a reappearance as the B-side to *1999*. Prince said he was inspired by John Lennon while writing the song. It was covered by Cyndi lauper on *She's So Unusual*.

MC Hammer sampled the song for his hit single 'Pray'.

'When Doves Cry' stopped Bruce Springsteen's 'Dancing in the Dark' from reaching number one.

Prince's biographer Per Nilsen stated that the song was about Prince's relationship with Susan Moonsie of Vanity 6.

Engineer Peggy McCreary told *Billboard* that when Prince removed the bassline from the song he said to her, 'There's nobody that's going to have the guts to do this.'

Reporter for *Entertainment Weekly* Leah Greenblatt did a story on Paisley Park and at one point said, 'Yes, he keeps doves. Yes, they cry.' Neighbours stated that Paisley Park was very quiet, 'Except for the doves.'

Prince played every instrument on the song.

Patti Smith recorded a version of the song. It was used in the soundtrack for the Sofia Coppola film *Lost in Translation*.

The music video was directed by Prince and featured a flock of doves, Prince in a bathtub, shots from the film *Purple Rain* and performances by The Revolution.

McCreary also recalled, 'It was the longest I ever worked with anybody in my life. I worked around the clock, 24 hours. He said sometimes the only reason he went home was so I could sleep.'

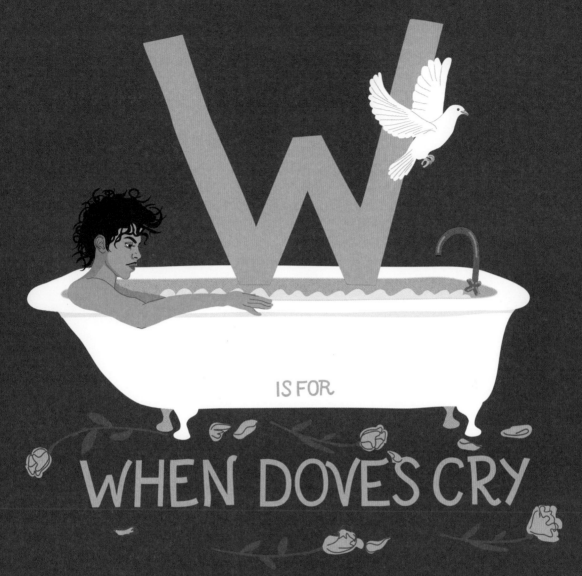

W

IS FOR

WHEN DOVE'S CRY

One of Prince's signature tunes, 'When Dove's Cry' was the lead single from *Purple Rain*, released in May, 1984. Surely the best song ever written about how it feels to be in a relationship and fighting all the time, the pain and frustration seeps through every note. Who but Prince would reference the sweet-sounding coo of a dove, reimagining the sound in distress to make you really feel the song's theme. 'When Doves Cry' went to number one in America and several other countries around the world. It was certified platinum at a time when that meant selling two million copies, and it ranked at number 52 in *Rolling Stone's* 500 greatest songs of all time. *Billboard* ranked it the number one song of 1984. After Prince's death, the song re-entered the chart at number eight. The song is distinguished by the complete absence of a bassline (similar to 'Kiss'), and the intro is instantly recognisable by the 'metal' guitar lead riff, followed by the stark drum-machine beat.

X IS FOR X-RATED

While he might have claimed to have spent his later Jehovah's Witness years in celibacy, for most of Prince's career, sex was an integral part of his art. Sexual expression (alongside religion) was the over-arching theme in his writing. In an era when the AIDS epidemic was producing a climate of fear surrounding sex, Prince was openly celebrating sex and sexuality, urging his audience to get off, cream, come, orgasm, get head and to let Prince himself 'fuck the taste out of your mouth'. Despite his reserved public persona, in his videos and onstage his performance persona would writhe, cavort and simulate sex acts. Add his gender fluidity and dazzling fashion to this and you get material that is ripe for controversy. Prince's private persona is somewhat of a mystery, but, unsurprisingly, plenty of unreliable witnesses stepped forward after his death with lurid stories of his sexual exploits.

Ex-girlfried Charlene Friend alleged that Prince was living on a 'cocaine diet' and would have 'wild, sex-themed parties' in special rooms that had chains, whips and cages. Friend claimed that he filmed her without consent and told her that he wanted her 'on call'. Prince denied all of these allegations.

The Prince 12" *Scandalous Sex Suite*, recorded when he was dating Kim Basinger, is said to contain the actress's sex noises.

Prince and Apollonia's coupling in the film *Purple Rain* played more like a Prince music video than an actual sex scene, and has often been described as one of the most laughable sex scenes in cinema history (although it has been stated that it was heavily edited to avoid an X rating).

Ex *Playboy* model Anna Fantastic, who Prince dated when she was 18, opened up the Prince sex files in an article for *The Sun*. She described him as an amazing lover, but not into kinky stuff. He even told her that he didn't want her to be in *Playboy*.

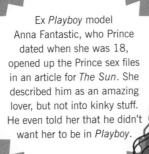

Among Prince's more X-rated lyrics were from 'Jack U Off': 'I'll jack u off / I only do it for a worthy cause / Viriginity or menopause / U'll have an instant heart attack if I jack u off'. From 'Head': 'I'll give u head / Til u're burning up / Head / Til u get enough / Head / Til your love is red / Head love til you're dead'. And from 'Do Me Baby': 'Take me baby, kiss me all over / Play with my love / Bring out what's been in me 4 far 2 long'.

Xpectation
Released on January 1st, 2003, *Xpectation* was Prince's 26th studio album. Mostly instrumental, *Xpectation* came out just two weeks after Prince's piano and voice album *One Nite Alone...* As a digital release only, the album wasn't available for the charts. Every track on the album begins with the letter 'x': 'Xhalation, Xcogitate', 'Xemplify', 'Xpectation', 'Xotica', 'Xogenous', 'Xpand', 'Xosphere' and 'Xpedition'.

...

'Xenophobia'
This track made its appearance on the live version of *One Nite Alone...* but wasn't included on the studio album. The album *Xpectation* was originally going to be called *Xenophobia*, with this track as the lead, but instead it was removed from the album entirely. 'Xenophobia' cropped up again when Prince used it as the title for his Paisley Park Studios shows. Called *Xenophobia Celebration*, Prince performed a live show every day for a week in June 2002. A bootleg 12-CD set exists, with recordings of the whole event.

...

Xylophone
Prince (or possibly Sheila E.), played Xylophone on the song 'Play in the Sunshine,' the second track on the album *Sign o' the Times*. Prince also wrote a track called 'Xylophone', an instrumental that was most likely intended to have appeared on *Xpectation*, but didn't make the final cut. A 26-second snippet from the track was streamed on The NPG Music Club website for a short while.

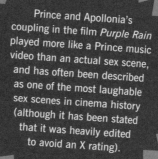

y

IS ALSO FOR

#YesWeCode

After the fatal shooting of unarmed African American high-school student Trayvon Martin, and the subsequent aquittal of his shooter, Prince worked together with political activist and commentator Van Jones to launch an initiative that teaches young people of colour to code. Jones said, 'After the Trayvon Martin verdict I was talking to Prince and he said, "You know, every time people see a young black man wearing a hoodie, they think, he's a thug. But if they see a young white guy wearing a hoodie they think, oh that might be Mark Zuckerberg. That might be a dot-com billionaire."' After his death, the organisation posted on their website, '#YesWeCode would like to honor Prince and thank him for his inspired vision for #YesWeCode. Prince's commitment to ensuring young people of color have a voice in the tech sector continues to impact the lives of future visionaries creating the tech of tomorrow.'

...

Yo La Tengo

Dump, a side project for Yo La Tengo's bass player James McNew, recorded a mini album of Prince covers called *That Shiny Motherfucker With the High Voice*.

...

'Yo Mister'

Prince wrote this song for Patti LaBelle, who included it on her 1989 LP, *Be Yourself*. Prince also played various instruments, contributed backing vocals and produced the track, which reached number six on the US R&B chart.

In June 2016, Prince's yellow cloud guitar sold at auction to the owner of the Indianapolis Colts, Jim Irsay, for US$137,500. Irsay owns many guitars including ones previously owned by members of the Beatles.

Prince's Galpin Blvd home was painted yellow with purple trim.

Prince owned a bright yellow 1991 BMW 850 which appeared in clips for both 'Sexy MF' and 'Gangster Glam'.

In 2010, Prince recorded a fight song for the Minnesota Vikings, named for the team's colours – and his own – 'Purple and Gold'.

An album of rarities and unreleased demos called *Yellow* has been a popular Prince bootleg, and Sheila E.'s album *Romance* featured a song called 'Yellow', written by Prince.

Prince's 1992 *Vogue* profile describes that during the photoshoot, 'It was suggested that Prince wear his new taxi–yellow shiny PVC bolero and high-waisted tango jumpsuit, with yellow zipped shoes and matching guitar, of course.' Apparently not feeling the yellow that day, Prince told photographer Herb Ritts, 'Tell me if this makes you want to puke, throw up.' He then mysteriously walked off set telling Ritts to 'burn those negatives'.

While Prince will always be The Purple One, standing forever in the purple rain and living all his purple life riding purple bikes, at one point in his later career he flirted with another signature hue – yellow. Yellow, or gold, is opposite purple on the colour wheel, making them complementary colours and hence an obvious choice for Prince. He had one of his cloud guitars made in yellow and often played it while wearing a yellow button up jumpsuit, a yellow suit with Spanish frill shirt or a full yellow three-piece suit. At the Apollo Theater's 75th Anniversary Gala Concert, Prince took to the stage wearing a yellow suit with gold trim – complete with yellow pump shoes and yellow walking stick.

IS FOR
YELLOW

Z IS FOR JAY Z

Despite being one of the first artists to sell his music over the internet in 1997, in 2010, following frustrations at the way artists were losing out through piracy and platforms like iTunes, Prince declared that the internet was 'completely over'. He was still devoted to exploring new ways to distribute his music, so when Jay Z launched his own subscription-based music streaming service, Tidal – which promised higher percentages of royalties paid to artists and writers – Prince famously pulled all of his recordings from Spotify and other streaming services in favour of the new artist-friendly Tidal. Having spent much of his career fighting for both artistic and financial independence from record labels, artist-run distribution was a pursuit close to his heart. According to NPR, Prince said, 'Once we have our own resources, we can provide what we need for ourselves … Jay Z spent $100 million of his own money to build his own service. We have to show support for artists who are trying to own things for themselves.'

In a press conference promoting the Tidal service Prince said, 'I would tell any young artist … don't sign record deals.'

On Prince's birthday in 2016, Tidal added 15 more Prince albums including *The Black Album* and *Crystal Ball*.

In his rap over the Fat Joe and Remy Mar track 'All the Way Up' (exclusive to Tidal) Jay Z raps, 'they'll be forever protected' and makes reference to the Vault, 'Prince left his masters where they safe and sound / We never gonna let the elevator take him down'.

Reports state that Prince, alongside Beyonce, Kanye, Rhianna, Daft Punk, Arcade Fire and more, were given a stake in the company in exchange for their catalogues. At the launch they gathered onstage and were introduced as the 'Owners of Tidal.'

Tidal had an estimated three million subscribers by May 2016, in no small part due to it being the only place to stream Prince's music online.

TIDAL

According to *Billboard*, Prince said of Jay Z, 'And when we win on this, none of us'll gloat. He's not the gloating type anyway. He's slick with his. He says to brush the dirt off your shoulder.'

After Prince's death, Jay Z wrote through his Tidal page, 'A genius, innovator, creator, family member, Prince will be truly missed.' The message contained a link to Prince's Tidal page.

Z IS ALSO FOR

Bobby Z.
A member of The Revolution from 1978–1986, Robert Rivkin, better known by his stage name, Bobby Z., is a multi-instrumentalist who specialises in the drums. Prince and Bobby Z. re-united onstage in 2013 and Bobby Z. sat in on drums for 'Purple Rain' during the 3rdeyegirl shows. In 2014, Bobby Z. described recording the iconic song to *The Current* as, 'just one of those moments, as a band, that you live for … He calls it medicine, and it is; it just really has something about it, the way it crescendos, the way it crashes, and the way the guitar solo takes you to a place where you just feel different about your life. No matter what, when you hear those opening chords of 'Purple Rain', you just stop time somehow, and just listen…'

…

David Z.
Bobby Z's older brother was a producer in Minneapolis who worked extensively on Prince's recordings. The most famous input was as writer, producer and engineer on Prince's 1986 hit 'Kiss'. He helped shaped the minimalist and highly influential sound of the single.

…

Zodiac
Prince was a Gemini, born on June 7, and he often referred to the duality of his star sign in his lyrics. In 'My Name is Prince' he says: 'I've got two sides and they're both friends.' He told Oprah, 'Analysis has proved that there's probably two people inside of me. Just like Gemini, and we haven't determined what sex the other person is yet.' Prince also battles an archenemy named Gemini in a three-issue DC Comics series created by Dwayne McDuffie, called *Prince: Alter Ego*.

Smith Street Books

Published in 2017 by Smith Street Books
Melbourne | Australia
smithstreetbooks.com

ISBN: 978-1-925418-38-5

The moral right of the author has been asserted.
CIP data is available from the National Library of Australia.

Publisher: Paul McNally
Project editor: Hannah Koelmeyer, Tusk studio
Design: Michelle Mackintosh
Illustration: Alice Oehr

Printed & bound in China by C&C Offset Printing Co., Ltd.

Book 26
10 9 8 7 6 5 4 3 2 1